*THE HIGHER LEARNING
THE UNIVERSITIES
AND THE PUBLIC*

THE STAFFORD LITTLE LECTURES
AT PRINCETON UNIVERSITY, 1968

THE HIGHER LEARNING THE UNIVERSITIES AND THE PUBLIC

BY CARL KAYSEN

PRINCETON UNIVERSITY PRESS
PRINCETON, NEW JERSEY
1969

PREFACE

THE FIRST TWO CHAPTERS of this small book contain the text of the two Stafford Little lectures for 1967-68, substantially as I delivered them on February 6 and 8, 1968, with only a few changes in wording on editorial grounds. The Afterword presented in the final pages was added at the suggestion of the editors of the Princeton University Press as a way of indicating the lines along which I myself would answer the main question raised in the lectures.

I wish here to express my thanks to President Goheen and the Faculty Committee on Public Lectures of Princeton University for giving me the stimulus to formulate my ideas on these matters, and for their hospitality to me when I aired them. I am equally indebted to Princeton University Press and its Director, Herbert S. Bailey, Jr., for enabling me to put these thoughts into print. The thoughts themselves are the product of a long period of concern with the problems of the economics and politics of science, particularly in the course of participating for some years in the seminar on Science and Public Policy at the (then) Littauer School of Harvard University. Without attributing to them either responsibility for or agreement with what I say here, I wish to record my debt to my colleagues in that seminar, especially Don K. Price and Harvey Brooks.

C. K.

November 1968

1

THIS ESSAY examines the social functions of the American university in relation to its basis of financial support. For nearly the whole of this century the rate of growth of higher education has been high and fairly steady. Enrollments have marched ahead, old institutions have grown in size and scope, and new ones have been created. The cumulative growth over the whole period and the rapid rise in unit costs since the war have outstripped traditional sources of income and forced the universities to rely increasingly on public funds, especially federal funds. University administrators expect this reliance to grow even greater in the future, chiefly because they see no alternative.

It is my thesis that the basis on which much of the growing support from the public treasury has been asked and given in recent years does not correspond to what the universities are actually doing. This departure is most important in relation to the central institutional structures of modern universities, those that are most intimately con-

3

cerned with the higher learning itself. The nature of our governmental processes is such that a discrepancy of this sort cannot long persist. Some readjustment in the relation between the universities and their public sources of support which brings the purposes of donors and recipients together is inevitable, whether in the direction of finding new bases for support, or new uses for funds, or both.

It is now a commonplace to say that the university is a centrally important institution in the contemporary United States, and that it performs a wide variety of functions in response to a wide variety of clienteles. Clark Kerr, in his influential Godkin Lectures of 1963, coined the felicitous—if hardly euphonious—epithet "multiversity," to characterize this situation.

In speaking of "the university," I use the phrase in part as a shorthand for the whole system of higher education and, in part, in its proper sense. It is worth a moment's digression to sketch the place of the universities proper in the whole of the system of higher education. At the beginning of the 1965 academic year, there were more than 2,200 institutions describing themselves as institutions of higher education, ranging in character from great universities to junior colleges and schools of art and music. Altogether, they enrolled 5.6 million full-time degree candidates. Fewer than one in ten of these institutions had any sizable enrollment of students at the graduate level, beyond the four-year degree. Only 150 odd can be described as universities in the sense of offering some kind of advanced professional training and graduate work in academic subjects. If the distinguishing characteristic of the true university is taken to be the training of scientists and scholars and the production of serious work in science and scholarship, then their number is much smaller. Indeed, no more than three dozen institutions, currently accounting for nearly two-thirds the total output of Ph.D. degrees, constitute the body of American universities in this definition which is central to our concern with the higher learning. This number has clearly grown in the last generation, but far more slowly than the rates of growth in the activity of the whole system.

The social functions of the system of higher education can be considered for our purposes in terms of four categories. Some of these functions are performed by several types of institutions of higher education, some by institutions outside the formal educational system, although usually closely linked to it. The representative American university today performs all of them. The first category is the creation of new knowledge and its integration into the present body of knowledge in the widest sense. In this context I use "knowledge" to cover the whole range of organized cognitive activity: mathematics; the natural sciences; the social sciences; and the humanities including, increasingly, the fine arts. The two aspects of this function—the creation of new knowledge and its integration into the existing body in a situation of rapid growth in the total social stock of knowledge—are deeply intertwined. What is sometimes referred to as the preservation of learning is better viewed as the incorporation of new knowledge into the total stock, and therefore as inseparable from the creation of new knowledge.

The next function of the university is the transmission of knowledge to the new generation. This has two aspects which, though substantially overlapping, are worth distinguishing. The first is the transmission of general culture, what we usually call education as distinct from training. The second is the transmission of the varieties of expert knowledge relevant to the training of specialists. Universities in different times and places have differed in the extent to which they perform these two functions. They have almost always had some responsibility for whatever general education at an advanced level society provided; but usually offered it to only a small segment

6

of the population. Of the varieties of experts, only theologians have come near to being trained chiefly by the institutions of higher learning in most times and places. The training of experts is an increasingly important part of the total function in American higher education. More than one-half of the first college degrees earned in 1964-65 were in professional and vocational fields, and almost one-half of these, in turn, were in areas outside the older learned professions, even if education and engineering are included with the more traditional trio of medicine, law, and divinity. At the graduate level, professional degrees and masters' and doctors' degrees in professional and technical subjects are four times as numerous as higher degrees in the academic fields. Further, of course, the Doctors of Philosophy in the natural sciences, social sciences and humanities who staff the universities are, in our society, viewed as another type of specialist, however they see themselves. All in all, in the system as a whole, two out of every three degree recipients at every level are primarily the recipients of expert training, rather than of general education.

The third function of our institutions of higher learning is the application of knowledge to the solution of "practical" problems in the wider society. This activity, too, is now particularly characteristic of the universities, though it is hardly a new function. Land grant colleges and their associated agricultural stations were the earliest American examples. Today, almost every faculty in a modern university is associated with some enterprise of a problem-solving sort, from the design of complex weapons to the remodeling of the inner city slums. So are a high proportion of the professors, working as individuals, as consultants to governments, business firms, and foundations.

The final role of the higher educational system is the socialization of late adolescents and young adults, teaching them how to fit into the social roles they will fill as adults. This is closely connected with the transmission of culture, but distinct from it, dealing rather with the formation of values and habits, the selection of life styles, and the making of friendships, than with cognitive knowledge.

Each of these activities has, so to speak, its own particular market, in that it is directed more to one than another segment or stratum of the whole society. The markets for the application of knowledge to social problem-solving and those for the transmission of expert knowledge are closely related, and correspond to the relevant appropriate functional segments of society. Scientists and engineers who conceive new weapons for the Department of Defense and its contractors on one side of this process are, on the other, training the engineers who will reduce these conceptions to practice, produce them, and in some cases even help man the final product. The same parallel can be drawn for the economist who acts as a governmental adviser, and trains the specialists who will staff the Treasury, the Board of Governors of the Federal Reserve System, or the Bureau of the Budget.

The transmission of general culture is closely bound up with the activity of socializing the young. At an earlier time in our own history, and even more in the history of universities in other Western countries—when the production of experts and expertise played a far less important part than it now does—the transmission of general culture and the socialization processes that accompanied it were directed substantially at the same target group, a social elite connected with the ruling groups in the society. In no society, including our own, was higher education the sole means of socializing future members of the elite, but it played an important part in all. In the United States today, the transmission of general culture at the university level is a rapidly diminishing part of this process of socialization. On the other hand, some kind of advanced education, general or specialist, is increasingly a prerequisite to member-

9

ship, not just in a small elite, but in the wide middle class of an advanced industrial society. We may say that in the United States today, and increasingly in the future, the public served by this aspect of the process of higher education is the whole middle class of our society. Some higher education is already a nearly-indispensable ticket of entrance to middle-class status for boys of working-class origins. It will soon become only somewhat less indispensable to the maintenance of that status for those who were born into it.

The question of who provides the market for the activity of maintaining and increasing the stock of knowledge covered by the phrase "science and learning" is, of course, the central problem to which I am addressing myself. The first short answer is that it is chiefly the university itself, and this may indeed be the heart of the problem.

None of these four functions of the system of higher education is either totally new, or peculiar to the United States. The transmission of general culture and the socialization of an elite have been the function of universities all over the Western world for the last century and a half. So, to perhaps a lesser extent, has been the training of at least some kinds of experts, especially priests, doctors, and lawyers. The involvement of the university in practical problem-solving is more nearly

10

an American contribution, but one that dates back a century to the Morrill Act, and the land grant colleges. But despite these continuities in the individual elements, the present mixture is itself a significant novelty, differing both from the American past and the situation in other Western industrial countries. The element of novelty is provided by the particular combination of three factors: the wide range of involvement in practical problems and the correspondingly wide range of expertise which the university is asked to produce; the centrality of the devotion to science and learning in those universities that constitute the key element of the whole system; and, finally, the wide reach of the educational process throughout the whole of society. In the Fall of 1963, nearly one person in four in the United States population between the ages of 18 and 24 was enrolled as a full-time degree candidate in an institution of higher education. More than one in three of the 18 to 21-year olds were in undergraduate institutions or junior colleges. These proportions had more than doubled since the end of World War II. They have grown more than seven times over the last half-century.

Further, the reach of the educational system was far wider in the United States than in any other country in the world. There were nearly two students in higher education in the United States per 100 in population, and the number of those in the higher educational system was more than one-third of the number of those in secondary education. In the Soviet Union, Canada and Australia, which are closest to American practice, the proportion of the whole population in higher education was less than one-half that in the United States. In Canada and Australia, the ratio of students in colleges and universities to those in secondary schools was about one-third that of the United States, although in the Soviet Union the ratio was about the same. In the Western European countries, the corresponding proportions are smaller by another factor of two.

There is every prospect that the past high rates of growth in the size and scope of higher education in the United States will continue. Total enrollments are expected by the Office of Education to grow by almost 50 per cent from their current levels, reaching 9 million by 1975. It is noteworthy that the rate of growth of college enrollments in the past generation has been much greater than that of high school enrollments in the one that preceded it. This reflects, again, the proposition that some kind of higher education has increasingly become the passport to a middle-class occupation in an increasingly middle-class society.

The variety of practical involvements of the university and the corresponding variety of expert training it now provides can only be described as breathtaking. What Abraham Flexner, lecturing on "Universities, American, British, and German" at Oxford in 1950, held up for ridicule has become in some sense the characteristic American pattern. To be sure, not many great universities have schools of hotel management, but few or none are without involvement in laboratories of applied science and engineering, programs for reforming school curricula or institutes for reshaping urban building and traffic patterns. Unlike the school of hotel management, many of these activities deal with difficult problems of serious intellectual substance, and efforts to solve them generate new knowledge of the traditional academic kind. Some, of course, do not. The European university is still distant from this pattern, although some movement in this direction is discernible. In part, this difference reflects differences in academic structure. Engineering and applied science are largely the concern of separate technical institutions, rather than the university proper. The social sciences are relative newcomers to the European academic scene; attempts to apply them even newer. Even more important, however, is the rigid separation of government service from the universities and the business world. The highly professionalized permanent career government service of the European democracies is much less permeable to part-time and short-time academic visitors than our loose American structure. Much of the practical involvement of American universities began with problem-solving efforts for government purposes; European governments have only just begun to be willing to seek similar help.

Some measure of the growth of the significance of training experts is provided by the growth in graduate enrollments. The current level of some 700,000 is nearly six times what it was at the end of the Second World War; it is expected to reach one million by 1975, the level of the total college and university population two generations ago.

Perhaps the most significant change in the mixture is the central position that the cultivation of science and learning now occupies in our higher educational system, especially in the score or more great universities which form its core. It is in them, of course, that the bulk of the worthwhile scholarly and scientific work takes place. Their graduate schools train a large proportion of those who staff the whole system. Since those who did not go to these institutions usually wish they had, they provide the models for all the rest.

While the genuine cultivation of science and

14

learning at a serious level takes place at what is still a relatively small, though growing, number of institutions, its influence and ideal have spread rapidly. The prestige of identification with research and scholarship is sought increasingly throughout the system. Indeed, so powerful is the influence of the ideal that we see it turning up in the furthest corners of the system of higher education. Institutions above whose doors the legend "Teachers College" can still be discerned under the current label "State College" are already offering graduate work and doctors degrees. Within the true universities, those professors—usually the majority—who devote themselves to science and learning by way of their own work and the training of young scientists and scholars constitute the centers of power. Organized in departments along disciplinary lines, it is largely they (rather than administrators on the one hand or students on the other) who shape the character and purpose of the university. Departments exercise the major influence on course offerings and curricula, and these are increasingly conceived in terms of professional training in the discipline. The orientation and loyalty of the scholars are largely toward their professional colleagues around the nation and the world, rather than either toward the institution in which they work, or toward their students and

15

their roles as teachers. The rapid growth of the university system and the high competition among institutions for able men have led to an unprecedented degree of academic mobility. It is the disciplinary peer group that makes the judgments as to who is desirable and who should be sought by each institution in the competitive race. This, in turn, reinforces loyalty to the discipline and weakens further the attachment to the institution which, for many, is at best a temporary home. While these attitudes are strongest in the sciences and social sciences, they are penetrating the humanities as well, and, to a surprising extent, even the traditional professional schools. Medical schools are more oriented toward science than toward practice. Many leading law schools are moving toward an academic concern with the substantive problems of social science that underlie the law, as well as grappling with the legal process itself from the perspective of political scientists as much as that of lawyers and teachers of lawyers. It is Nobel prizes, not places on the All-American teams, that the university president counts today. Whether the alumni do the same is another question, to which I shall return.

This devotion to science and scholarship is, in my view, the most noteworthy of the changes which the American university has experienced in the last generation. As academics we, of course, think it right and proper; indeed, so much so, that we do not often pause to note how remarkable it is. In the past, even as recently as the 1930s and certainly in earlier periods, science and scholarship were secondary activities in American colleges and universities. The transmission of culture, the education of an elite, and the training of a relatively small number of experts in a few traditional fields were their central concerns. The Johns Hopkins of Gilman and the Chicago of Harper were the exceptions, not the rule. Nor was it too much different in other countries. In England, on whose great universities the American College was modeled, scholarship and science were, until the most recent years, pursued essentially as private concerns by an academic community whose primary function lay in teaching. Only in nineteenth-century Germany was the pursuit of science and learning explicitly given the central place in the university. We can mention some of the important contributory factors to this result: the competition between the German states in the creation and support of universities that were entirely state-supported; the special impulse that Prussia felt after its defeats at the hands of Napoleon to create something new and excellent; perhaps sheer good fortune in the choice of the Prussian ministers of education at the beginning of this period; the fact that the universities dealt with a small elite. The organizational system of the universities themselves, with its elite corps of professors, each in complete command of research and study in his subject at his own institution, and its army of free-enterprise Privatdozenten aspiring for the vacant chairs that might become available during their careers and laboring for the achievement that would assure their selection in the competitive race, certainly gave a powerful impulse to scholarship and science.

The American graduate school was, in its origins, modeled after the German university. Yet it was not really until three generations after the first beginnings that the new institution became the central institution of the American system, and then in social circumstances differing as widely as one can possibly conceive from those in which the original operated. The new central importance of science and scholarship rested on a foundation of Federal money, provided chiefly in support of research and associated graduate training in the natural sciences. In 1963-64, the most recent year for which comprehensive figures of the financial accounts of higher education are available, total Federal support for current costs of educational activities of colleges and universities amounted to about $2.1 billion, of which $1.8 billion was used for the support of research, graduate training and related activities. These dollar totals represented 26 and 21 per cent, respectively, of total current expenditures for higher education. For the private institutions, which include a disproportionate share of graduate enrollment, and of the best universities, the corresponding figures were $1.1 and $1.0 billion, and the corresponding shares 31 and 29 per cent. This form of Federal support has grown very rapidly since the Second World War. Although figures comparable to those cited above are not available for this period, a closely related series, for Federal expenditures for basic research at universities, shows a twelvefold growth from 1953 to 1966. This growth was somewhat more rapid in the second half of the period, between 1957 and 1964. Since 1964, it has slowed down sharply.

The bulk of this support goes to a relatively small number of institutions, mostly the universities, and especially the quality universities which I have characterized as the central core of the system. In terms of their accounts, then, the proportionate importance of Federal research money is far greater than for higher education as a whole. While no figures are published, a guess would put the figures for this group at more like 50 than 30 per cent.

The initial impulse to Federal support of research resulted from the role of scientists in the Second World War, most spectacularly in the creation of nuclear weapons, but also in the development of radar, the refinement of submarine warfare, the development of penicillin, and many other applications. American academic science, immeasurably strengthened by the Europeans whom Hitler had driven out, revolutionized the technology of warfare. As a result of this experience, many public officials—including some, but not all of the leaders of the military services—believed that the continued support of science was an important national task. The first attempt to crystallize this sentiment was Vannevar Bush's report to the President in 1945, entitled *Science: The Endless Frontier*. Bush, the leader of the Office of Scientific Research and Development, which had organized the war work of science, argued the case for the institutionalization in peacetime of the government's support of science in the form of a national research foundation. The effort he envisaged was modest, beginning with a first year budget of $33 million, a third of which would be devoted to military research, and rising to a total expenditure of $120 million in five years, of which

20

only a sixth would be for military purposes. His effort did not meet with success until five years later, when the National Science Foundation was created in 1950. In the interim, however, the military services, especially the Office of Naval Research, and the Atomic Energy Commission continued to support academic science, in order to maintain capabilities which they thought vital to their missions. Their expenditures for academic science soon exceeded the scale that Bush had envisioned. The National Science Foundation, however, took ten years from 1950 to reach the level of spending Bush had foreseen in five. The impulses that had generated these activities were diminishing, and Federal expenditures on basic research had nearly ceased to grow, when they received a tremendous reinforcement by the Soviets' launching of the first man-made satellite in 1957. The pace of growth of Federal support for science, especially physical science, jumped and remained high for the next seven years. All during this period, there was a more-or-less unquestioned assumption that what was good for science was good for defense, and that increasing support of basic research and advanced training in the physical sciences would translate itself more or less proportionately into increasing military capabilities.

Beginning somewhat later, the biological sci-

21

ences were the beneficiaries of an increasing flow of support, provided chiefly by the National Institutes of Health. From the mid-fifties, a rapidly growing current of research funds for the support of biology, biochemistry, and to a small extent psychology, flowed to the nation's colleges and universities. In this case the impulse came from the Congress rather than the Executive, but the basic argument for providing research funds was analogous. For the decade before the pace of increase in research support slackened off, there was no tendency to question the assumption that more research would result in better health for the public, in rough proportion to the expenditures for research.

So far the natural sciences have received almost all the funds. Direct Federal support for research in the social sciences is minuscule, of the order of 5 per cent of total expenditures for the support of basic research. In the traditional fields of scholarship outside of science, there is only the smallest beginning of Federal support. With the creation of the National Endowment for the Humanities in 1964, the possibility of support is, at least, given institutional form, if still only token amounts of money.

These enormous differences in the degree of support by the Federal government for the different kinds of science and learning reflect the implicit rationale of the whole effort. In every case support rested primarily on the utilitarian argument that new knowledge was an essential input for the production of some socially desirable good or service, and that only the Federal Government could and would pay the great costs involved. These arguments were most easily accepted and least examined in regard to support for the physical sciences in relation to the national defense and military power of the United States, only slightly less so for the biological sciences and the improvement of the health of the public. The social sciences have only recently come into the field of consideration as having potential practical utility, and the traditional fields of humanistic learning still remain without the same kind of practical justification.

The organizational form in which federal support of science has been cast is as remarkable as the level and rate of growth of the support itself. Aside from money for research facilities, most of the support of science is given on the basis of competitive merit as judged by the scientific community itself. The bulk of the money for the direct support of research is allocated under the project system. Individual scientists and groups of scientists in the universities and in other research

23

institutions apply for the support of research projects. These applications are examined and graded by advisory committees of leading scientists in the appropriate disciplines who work on a part-time basis as consultants to the grant-making agencies. Agencies themselves follow the advice of their expert panels within the constraints of their budgets.

To be sure, determinations of the relative support of different branches of science are made through traditional governmental processes. In part, the direct action of Congress in setting up programs defines the kind of science that will be supported. Thus, for example, the rapid growth of expenditures by the National Institutes of Health has led to a redressing of the earlier imbalance in favor of the physical, rather than the biological, sciences. This, in turn, reflected the conceptions of the Department of Defense, the Atomic Energy Commission and the National Science Foundation early in its history as to what kind of science should be supported. In part, these determinations on relative support come from the Executive branch, where they are, of course, heavily influenced by the structure of advisory committees, typically staffed by leading academic scientists. For example, there has recently been an examination of support for oceanography, meteorology, geophysics, and other "environmental sciences"

24

within the Federal establishment, which has led to a substantial increase for these fields compared with their earlier position in relation to more abstract physical sciences.

Within these broad governmental determinations of allocations among different fields of science the distribution of resources to individual projects and individual scientists is made, essentially, by the scientific community. This process is most formalized in the National Institute of Health and the National Science Foundation, but it operates in an essentially similar way within the other agencies as well. That part of the support of science which takes the form of fellowships for doctoral and postdoctoral training is similarly subject to a competitive process in which the judgments of advisory panels drawn from the scientific community are central.

Viewed as a process of public administration, this system is unique. There is no other large government program which leaves decisions on resource allocations in the hands of the community of beneficiaries explicitly and specifically, rather than maintaining it within the control of the government agencies themselves. The very uniqueness of the arrangement may be a source of instability in it.

From the point of view of science, this system

is widely admired as encouraging the maintenance of quality in research and avoiding ignorant bureaucratic interference in the substance of science. It also, of course, has the effect of supporting the power of the community of professionals—the professor and his peers—as against the power of the educational institution and its administrators. The organizational framework it provides reinforces the orientation of the academic scientist to his profession and his colleagues, enhances his possibilities of mobility, and diminishes his concern with those aspects of the academic world which lie outside research and graduate training.

Although only the sciences, especially the natural sciences, have been the beneficiaries of the federal largesse, the same organizational tendencies have spread beyond them to the whole of academic life. Forces of competition between universities and equity within them have extended to the less well-financed social sciences and to some degree even to the impoverished humanities the same patterns that have developed in the natural sciences.

In recent years, the rate of growth of federal spending on science has slowed down sharply. Total expenditures for research and development of all kinds have almost stopped growing. The small part of this total represented by expenditures on basic academic research has continued to grow, but no longer at the 15 to 20 per cent per year rates of the preceding decade. A number of forces external to science account for this slowdown. The major one, of course, is the pressure of other budgetary demands in a total Federal Budget which is still growing rapidly; most immediate, of course, is the effect of the Vietnam War. Further, the fact that by 1964 the share of research and development expenditures in the Federal budget had reached 15 per cent, compared with more like 1 per cent in the immediate post-war period, itself invites a closer scrutiny of the demands for more in both the Executive and Congressional processes of budget-making. This process has led to a more explicit examination within the government of the justifications for continued growth in the Federal support of academic science. In turn, there has been an increasingly alarmed response from the leaders of academic science who are concerned by the slowdown which they see as an immediate threat to the health of science.

A symptomatic and characteristic governmental example of this pressure was the action of the House Committee on Science and Astronautics when, in 1964, it addressed to the National Academy of Science a request for answers to two following questions:

27

"1. What level of Federal support is needed to maintain for the United States a position of leadership through basic research in the advancement of science and technology and their economic, cultural, and military applications?"

and

"2. What judgment can be reached on the balance of support now being given by the Federal Government to various fields of scientific endeavor, and on adjustments that should be considered, either within existing levels of overall support or under conditions of increased or decreased overall support?"

That a Committee of the House which, as much as any other, had been an enthusiastic supporter of the growing Federal support of research should ask these questions was indicative of the feeling within the government that no fully satisfactory rationale for the Federal science program had been offered, and that, without one, the continued growth of the program was in danger.

The questions were characteristic in two ways. First, they were addressed to the National Academy, which institutionalized, so to speak, the interests of the beneficiaries of the program. This mode of procedure is not peculiar to Federal sup-

28

port of science. The ability of beneficiaries or their spokesmen to justify government programs directed to them has always been a test of their survival value in the American political process. Since the Committee and the Academy stand in the typical client-patron relationship that marks the representatives of an organized (more or less) interest group and the substantive Committees of the Congress which deal with legislation concerning them, this was to be expected. Also characteristic is the assumption implicit in the language of the first question, that an answer to it can be offered in utilitarian terms.

The response to this Congressional inquiry took the form of a volume entitled *Basic Research and National Goals*, containing fifteen essays, mostly by leading natural scientists, addressing themselves to the issues. Perhaps an even more representative response of the scientific community to these pressures is provided by a series of studies examining needs and opportunities in the major branches of science. These, which are still under way, also under the auspices of the National Academy, are the work of panels of distinguished members of the several disciplines, selected chiefly from among the Academy's members. Studies on physics, chemistry, astronomy and several fields of biology have already appeared, and further studies

29

covering other branches of science are in preparation. Each study combines a careful discussion of the current substantive problems of the science at a semipopular level, a history of growth in Federal support and in graduate instruction in the discipline, a projection of the future need for scientists in the field, and an estimate of required levels of future Federal support to meet the needs. Last year a series of similar surveys for the major fields of study in social sciences was initiated under the joint sponsorship of the National Academy of Science and the Social Science Research Council. These will undoubtedly follow a similar pattern and set forth a series of claims on Federal funds required to support the necessary growth of the social sciences.

A number of these estimates for individual sciences, as well as several for the overall growth needs of academic natural science as a whole, agree in picturing the near future need, defined in these terms, as requiring at least a continuation of past rates of increase of Federal support; some point to a need for even more. This poses sharply the question to which I address myself: is the rationale on which this support has been granted sufficiently clear and persuasive to sustain its continued or even increased growth?

Before we examine the grounds that have been

given for the Federal support of science in order to see whether they are likely to be adequate to bear the continuing weight which is asked of them, we must remind ourselves, briefly, of the general context in which decisions on resource allocation are made in our society. By and large, we rely on the market mechanism to determine how economic resources are used. The rule of the market mechanism, of course, is that people pay for what they get, and can and will, within broad limits, get anything that they are prepared to pay for. If what people are prepared to pay for a good does not cover the costs of supplying it, it will disappear from the market. We recognize, of course, that some needs are not met by this mechanism, and these we look to the government to provide. We rely on government, rather than the market, to provide goods and services which have a large element of collective benefit. Some, like national defense and clean air, are truly collective goods in that no single individual can vary the level of his use of them independently of others. Some, like education, can be enjoyed in varying amounts by different persons, but they contain a large additional element of spillover, so that the society as a whole, as well as the particular individual who receives the education, enjoys the benefits, at least up to some level of education. There are also spe-

31

cial functions which we think of as uniquely governmental and whose character would change if they were not publicly provided, for example the administration of justice, but they are not significant in economic terms.

In addition to allocative decisions which affect the use of resources directly, the government, of course, engages in many activities whose aim is income redistribution. Dissatisfactions of politically powerful groups with the income distribution resulting from the market mechanism induce corrective governmental actions. These two categories may not suffice to explain every governmental activity that is observed in practice, but they provide an underlying rationale for distinguishing appropriate governmental activities in a market economy. Some activities of government, of course, contain purposes of both kinds, and every change in resource allocation involves some change in income distributions and vice versa. However, it seems more appropriate to consider governmental support of science and learning as coming under the first, rather than the second, purpose.

In this framework three different kinds of arguments can be made to justify the view that the cultivation of science and learning confers benefits which cannot be paid for through the market mechanism and which are spread sufficiently broadly that Federal support of them is justified. We can call them the utilitarian, the cultural, and the pyramid-building arguments.

The utilitarian argument is most typically made to justify publicly government support of research on a large scale. It is the argument scientists use to the community at large, that government officials responsible for the administration of Federal programs in science make to the Congress, and that the Congress, in effect, has endorsed by its legislation and appropriations. There are at least two parts of the utilitarian argument worth distinguishing. The first is that new scientific knowledge is an essential input to activities which the government itself characteristically undertakes. The most important of these is national defense, but others are public health and space exploration. The Federal government, having undertaken on broad political grounds to improve the public health, becomes responsible for providing the resources needed for new basic biological knowledge on which the improvements in public health themselves rest. Similarly, having made a political decision for reasons of international prestige to support a large-scale program of space exploration, the government must provide the wherewithal to produce the knowledge of solar astronomy, space physics and the like that is requisite to a successful program of space exploration.

It was, of course, this argument in respect to the importance of new scientific knowledge to military power which was the original stimulus for the whole process that we are examining. In all three cases, it can be said that since government is responsible for the activities for which new science is an essential input, it must see that the input is available.

The second part of the utilitarian argument justifies the support of basic science as an input to a number of activities which are the primary responsibility of other parts of the society than the Federal government. First among them is economic growth. New scientific knowledge is an indispensable input to new technology, and that new technology, in turn, is the chief stimulus to continuing economic growth. The development of new technology itself is financed primarily in the industrial sector by those firms that expect to benefit from its embodiment in new products and more efficient processes. When they succeed in producing marketable new products and useful new processes, they secure the benefits of them through patents, trademarks, brand acceptance and other marketing devices. Thus they can recover and justify the costs of research and development involved. New scientific knowledge, however, is a public good which is freely available to all and difficult or impossible for any one firm to keep for itself. The benefits of what any firm paid for would be available to its competitors without charge. For this reason, rational business firms operating on market motivations would not pay for an adequate amount of basic scientific research. But since all firms, and through them the whole economy, would benefit from more scientific knowledge, there is a case for Federal support of basic research.

The next activity for which research forms a vital ingredient is the training of technical specialists at an advanced level. The best kind of training for the professional practice in the application of the scientific disciplines is provided in a research atmosphere. This, typically, produces the combination of basic scientific understanding with versatility and flexibility in the use of that understanding to solve problems, that is most useful in applied science, development, and engineering. Since there is a growing need for both more and more highly trained experts and technicians of all sorts in a society in which technologies are growing more complex and changing rapidly, the increase in educational requirements calls for a corresponding increase in academic research. Unlike the preceding argument, this one

35

contains no explicit reason why the increasing volume of advanced training should be financed by the government. Implicit in it, however, is a return to the first argument above: that a large part of the new technical expertise is required in the service of defense, public health, or other governmental purposes.

Another branch of the utilitarian argument has become fashionable recently. It tends to be advanced more by academic administrators than by scientists, but it is also widely used within the government both in the Executive branch and the Congress. It is a mixture of the two preceding arguments and emphasizes both scientific research and the availability of technical manpower as stimuli to regional growth. Logically, it is more relevant to the geographic allocation of Federal support for science than to its level. However, in political terms, it functions as an argument for an increase in the total level, since it is easier to allocate more in absolute terms to previously disfavored localities and regions out of a rising total, than to take from one to give to another.

The cultural justification for government support of science and learning is typically used within the scientific community itself, though it is sometimes addressed to the rest of the world by the scientists. It figures only infrequently in the arguments used by administrators and politicians. In its most widely used form, the argument embodies the proposition that science is an especially valuable activity from the cultural point of view, that the advancement of knowledge is one of the ends of social life and that, in particular, the level of government support of advanced training and research should be such as to enable all who have the desire to do scientific work and the ability to carry it on on a useful level to do so. Particularly strong forms of the cultural justification are sometimes advanced. One holds that science is the characteristic cultural activity of our civilization: accelerators are the cathedrals of the twentieth century. Further, science is distinguished from other intellectual and cultural activities as producing results that are public and objective in character, as opposed to the private and subjective character of the knowledge produced by literature, the arts, and traditional philosophical knowledge. Another strong form of the cultural argument sees science as an activity of particular moral worth, so that an increase in scientific activity is, itself, an increase in the valuable achievement of society, irrespective of its particular results. In this view, work in science embodies some of the key values of our culture: individualism, respect for hard work and achievement, impersonality and objectivity, internationalism, and a belief in the potential equality of all men. A slightly different emphasis in the cultural argument, perhaps addressed more to the community at large than to the scientists themselves, is the proposition that excellence in science confers international prestige and that science is a measure of national achievement, independently of its contribution to military and economic strength.

The pyramid-building argument sees in science both a moral and an economic outlet for the aggressive and accumulative instincts of an industrial society. Science can become both the moral equivalent of war and the economic equivalent of war industry. On the one hand, it can give an outlet for competitive and aggressive impulses in the conquest of ignorance rather than of other nations. On the other, it can provide a kind of perpetual public works program which, like war industry, need never be satiated; like war industry, too, it creates a market for sophisticated products embodying advanced technologies. Together, both these functions provide a continuing and unfailing stimulus to economic growth.

All these arguments for government financial support apply in the first instance to the natural sciences, but some are, of course, capable of extension to other branches of science and learning. The cultural argument can equally well be appropriated by the social sciences which, among other things, may see in themselves the modern way to fulfilling the Platonic injunction. And, of course, it is the humanities which are the traditional claimants of the cultural justification for their existence. Utilitarian values are hard for the humanities to claim; indeed, the opposite is the case, and most advocates of the humanities reject them. But those parts of the utilitarian argument which refer to intellectual inputs for essential government functions and the training of technical experts can be claimed as well by the social as by the natural sciences. The role of economics in relation to effective governmental policy has now been recognized for so long as to be considered established. Increasingly, the claims of sociology, psychology, anthropology, and political science to supplying essential inputs to policy-making in the new areas of government policy are growing. These new areas of policy are simultaneously creating a growing demand for technical experts to man them. Only the claim for new scientific knowledge as an input to economic growth through improved technology is confined primarily to the natural sciences, and even here there may be dispute from the prophets of industrial sociology and psychology, who see possibilities of productivity increases from more effective cooperation as great as those from more efficient capital goods.

2

L ET US NOW EXAMINE in some detail the justifications that have been advanced for the public support of science and learning, which were summarized under the three headings, "utilitarian," "cultural," and "pyramid-building." Both the intellectual and the political limits of these arguments must be considered: To what extent are they right? To whom do they appeal, and how powerfully?

As academics, we have a duty to our calling not to advance arguments which we do not believe, even if they are appealing. And we have a common-sense responsibility to ourselves not to advance arguments which are ineffectual. In general, the utilitarian arguments prove in part unconvincing and in part insufficient, although they have been widely used and accepted in the past. The cultural and pyramid-building arguments score better on intellectual grounds, but they are unlikely to survive and function effectively in the political process of competition for budget resources.

43

The first utilitarian argument for supporting science is that it is an essential input to new technology, whether for the government or private sectors. The term "input" in this use is essentially metaphoric, and it carries with it the connotation of some fixed and definite relation to "outputs." The idea is that science is, so to speak, if not the ore from which new technology is smelted, at least the enzyme which is necessary for its synthesis, so that the rate of synthesis depends on the amount of available enzyme. But this is a misleading metaphor. A more helpful one would picture new science as a flow into a stock of organized scientific knowledge, and technology as drawing from that stock. The stock at any one time, however, is large relative to the flows both "in" and "out." Further, of course, the outflows do not diminish the stock in the usual sense: while the same invention cannot be made twice, the same scientific principle can be embodied in a multitude of different inventions. And once in the stock, the knowledge remains available at a cost that is essentially zero, measured in relation to the costs of acquiring it. This metaphor makes plainer one of the key aspects of the relations between science and technology, that there need be no close temporal connection between the flow of new scientific knowledge and the flow of new applications in technology. Such spectacular examples of very rapid translation of new science into new technology as the transistor and related solid-state devices must be balanced off against examples of lags of the order of a century, such as the applications of matrix algebra to aerodynamics and the analysis of communication networks.

The metaphor of the "stock" of scientific knowledge has its limitations too. "New science" is not merely, or even chiefly, an addition of more of the same to the existing stock. Frequently, and perhaps most importantly, it is a transformation of some larger or smaller part of the existing stock of knowledge. Thus the "size" of the stock bears no more simple relation to the inflow of new knowledge than it does to its outflow in technology.

It is clearly the case that the relation between science and technology is now closer in many fields than it was at an earlier period, certainly before the First World War, and probably before the Second. This is especially true in the realm of electronic, chemical, and medical technologies; it is becoming true in other fields as well. Further, this growing intimacy is in general more characteristic in the United States than in other Western industrial countries. This is in contrast with the whole period from the beginning of industrialization up to the 1920s, when most major develop-

45

ments in technology proceeded without close connection to the contemporary work of science.

This increasing intimacy between science and technology coincides with what appears to be some increase in the last two decades in the overall rate of technical progress in our economy, as measured by the growth in output per unit of inputs. But the increase is small, the problem of measuring it with any precision great, and it is too soon to say with confidence that a real change in the rate of technical progress is taking place.

Even if we accept the evidence as showing a real increase in the rate of technical change, its significance for our question of the relation between science and technology is ambiguous. First, there appears to be a step-up in the pace at which new technologies are introduced into the economy —the time between first conception and widespread use in practice. There has always been a significant spread between the most advanced available technology and that used by the average producer or embodied in the representative durable good. A narrowing of this spread results in a rise in the rate of progress, as long as it is going on. Such a movement is quite independent of the rate of first introduction of new technology.

Then, too, the recent period has shown a great increase in the efforts and resources put into applied science and development. These efforts are mostly distinct from the work of academic science directed at new understanding and new concepts, and they could be guiding new developments in technology without immediate dependence on new science.

Recently the Department of Defense made a study which aimed at measuring the relative contributions of what I have been calling academic science ("undirected science" in the study) and applied science and technology to the value of a sample of twenty new weapons systems introduced over the last two decades. The "value" in question was defined as the difference in cost of achieving the same results with each of the given systems, and the predecessors that they replaced. This study concluded that of all the innovations embodied in the new systems—as compared with the old—90 per cent were the products of applied science and technology of the previous twenty years directed specifically at improving weapons. The contribution of academic science could be measured in a fifty-year time scale, rather than in the twenty-year time scale of the study. The results of this study are consonant with the results of the few available similar studies that have been made in respect to industrial innovation in the civilian sector.

47

None of those observations is offered to deny that there is *some* relation between the growth of science and the development of technology. Rather their purpose is to illustrate the difficulties of quantifying the relation, especially in terms of the appropriateness of any particular rate of growth of scientific knowledge to the requirements of an advancing technology. Yet the translation of a general utilitarian argument that an increase in scientific knowledge will have useful practical consequences into terms which can justify some particular commitment of resources to the increase of knowledge requires just such quantification.

These difficulties are compounded by two further complexities of any justification of the support of science as an input to technology. The first is the fact that the different utilitarian arguments are not simply additive. The same body of new knowledge may be relevant to a variety of purposes, and serve as an input to several different kinds of uses. The new science that is relevant to the advance of weapons technology may not be different from the new science that is useful for developing new devices for the economy. The second, which is converse of the first, is that the sphere of usefulness of a particular item of new scientific knowledge is highly uncertain and difficult to foresee. This wide variability in area of application as well as in timing of potential benefits again makes difficult a division of responsibility—in financial terms—for different kinds of science to different functional areas of government in any consistent and exhaustive way.

At best, the sharpest correct statement that can be made in this branch of the utilitarian justification is that the increase in knowledge in the natural sciences, as a whole, is related, broadly, to an increase in the capability for producing new technology. But whether a doubling of the resources devoted to producing more academic science would double, or increase by only a little or simply not affect, the society's capability for technical advance over the next twenty years in some particular sector or in general, and conversely, whether halving them would halve it, or leave it unchanged, are questions that cannot be answered in terms of our present understanding and knowledge of the relations of science and technology.

Such are the perplexities that arise in considering the utilitarian arguments for the benefits of adding to our scientific understanding of nature. Different, and perhaps even more difficult obstacles lie in the path of a convincing practical justification of the systematic study of man and society. Whatever the relation between the development of natural science and that of technology, there exists within our society a well-defined and generally well-functioning mechanism for transforming potential technologies into actual ones—the business firm operating in the market. By and large, this mechanism works to realize the potential with a relatively low degree of slippage. Indeed, the argument can be made that it is too low; and that the potential social consequences of technical change that is economically profitable are too little reckoned in the balance.

Knowledge generated in the social sciences has its most important practical applications in government, and what is applied is determined chiefly through the workings of the political process. This is not a mechanism designed to use new knowledge readily; quite the opposite, it has a strong bias toward conservatism and inertia. This is neither surprising, nor necessarily undesirable. In the sphere of public policy, new modes of action tend to be bound up with at least the potentiality of new goals of policy. These in turn inevitably mean disturbances in the existing social and political equilibrium, and any system stable enough to survive will tend to resist such changes. Thus questions of the significant practical use of social science knowledge are always political questions, and will, rather than understanding, plays the key role. To say this is not to despair of the application of reason to

50

the problems of society, but simply to recognize that it is a slow and uncertain business. Its spread is controlled much more narrowly by the pace at which widely held values change on the one hand, and the pressures of unsolved problems on the other, than by the rate at which potentially useful knowledge can be generated.

The second branch of the utilitarian argument is that academic research is an indispensable ingredient of the advanced training of experts, including both the experts who will apply their knowledge to the practical problems of the larger society, and the much smaller fraction who will be the next generation of academic researchers and teachers. It is applicable over the whole field of natural and social science, and even to the humanities insofar as the training of the next academic generation goes. This proposition has one important advantage over the more widely used appeal to direct economic utility, it reflects the conviction based on personal experience of a large part of the relevant community of experts, both academic and non-academic, and in a matter in which the testimony of personal experience is both competent and weighty. Nonetheless, it cannot pass without some challenges. The first is again the difficulty of translating the general proposition into quantitative terms. How much involvement in what level of research is needed to turn out the competent specialist? On the other side, what proportion of his time and effort should the university professor be allowed to devote primarily to his researches or his most advanced students? Hard as it is to find a point of attack for a quantitative answer to these questions, it is clear that variations on the answers in a reasonable range make a significant difference to the costs involved.

The second challenge is the apparently successful functioning of quite different arrangements as to the relations of academic research and the advanced training of experts of all types. The polar opposite of our own system of increasing interpenetration of the two processes is exemplified in the Soviet Union, where universities and technical institutes are primarily responsible for training, and the various Institutes of the Academy of Sciences are responsible for academic research over the whole range of science and learning. The separation is by no means complete: members and corresponding members of the Academy do hold professorships and other teaching posts at the universities; the universities and technical institutes have research institutes attached to them which are not part of the Academy structure. But in principle, the two functions are organized and funded separately, each in terms of its own goals and purposes. The level of Soviet science and technology is not such, in comparison with that of the United States, as to argue the clear superiority of one or the other system.

What these observations point to is the difficulties of defending as right and necessary just the proportionate mixture of research and advanced training that has evolved over the last two decades, under the stimulus of a rapidly growing level of Federal support, concentrated in the natural sciences and the fields of application most closely related to them.

In relying on utilitarian arguments to justify growing Federal support of science and learning, the academic community may incur liabilities in addition to those of bad conscience. I asserted in my first chapter that erroneous arguments have a low survival value, in what is becoming an increasingly critical and rational process of governmental resource allocation at the Federal level. Yet, it can be urged, despite the argument I have presented so far, that for all their imprecision and lack of quantitative scale, there is enough sense in the utilitarian arguments to enable them to serve their political purpose. What this overlooks is the degree to which continued utilitarian justifications may create the demand for practically useful results, and so undercut the purpose of the whole enterprise. The Department of Defense's report quoted above is one example of this kind of pressure. Another is the recent impulses of both the Congress and the President to seek more "results" in terms of better health care from the Public Health Service, after more than fifteen years of rapidly growing appropriations for the support of research, both intramurally and at the universities.

To take a homely example, advances in plasma physics, in which members of both Princeton University and the Institute for Advanced Study have played an important part, had their origin about 15 years ago in a more euphoric era of research support, in an inquiry into the possibilities of converting the energy of nuclear fusion into electric power. It is not clear how much nearer that goal is; but our understanding of the behavior of plasma has been much advanced. Yet if the question of how to generate electric power had been pressed too hard by those who supported this research, it is doubtful that either the power or the knowledge would have been achieved.

The third type of utilitarian argument—the special impetus that research, the availability of trained manpower, and the proximity of a university give to local or regional development—can be dismissed as resting on nothing more than assertion. There simply is no logical reason to believe

54

that local demand generated by Federal dollars spent on these particular activities have a peculiar power to stimulate local development greater than that of equivalent demand for whatever outputs generated by Federal or other extra-regional sources. Nor does the little empirical evidence that has been studied suggest that anything has been overlooked in the usual general argument on this point.

On the other hand, to say this is not to deny that a Federal program under which, potentially, funds can be allocated to particular regions and localities has a solid political appeal, given the structure of the legislature and the nature of its committee processes. That funds for research facilities and research support can become a new rivers and harbors program is not at all unimportant for the future level of appropriations; the Congress has already displayed its keen interest in the geographic distribution of research funds. But, of course, this interest cuts across the interest of the scientific community in making grants on merit, as determined by the judgments of the community, and thus the appeal to regional development is a particularly dangerous one for the scientific community to espouse.

The cultural arguments for the support of science and learning cannot be examined in terms of

55

their validity in the same sense as the utilitarian ones just reviewed. They are statements of value, which can be described as aesthetic, or moral, and looked at in terms of internal consistency, or consistency with judgments of value in other spheres. The central proposition advanced in these arguments is that the level of support of science should be such as to provide for all willing and qualified workers. It has the virtue of providing, at least in principle, a measure of the appropriate level of support. Further, despite many problems of application in detail, the mechanism of criticism and collective evaluation that is built into the heart of the social processes of science provides a reasonably consistent scale for drawing the line of eligibility within each discipline. One can speak with much less confidence of the ability of this process to find the astrophysicist just worth supporting in relation to the sociologist just worth supporting; but in this respect, we are not clearly worse off with this criterion than with a utilitarian one.

What the cultural criterion lacks, of course, is political appeal. Science and learning, and especially that part of it which commands the widest and strongest admiration among the communities of its practitioners, is caviar to the general, too esoteric and difficult for sympathetic appreciation either by the 550 representative legislators or their

200 million constituents. Whatever the economics of the argument, science *is* technology, as far as American popular culture goes, and this is true up to quite high levels of popular culture. It is this which gives utilitarian arguments their vitality, as well as their dangers.

The stronger forms of the cultural argument are, of course, even less convincing. They assign special worth to the activities of a small group which the great bulk of the country finds incomprehensible. Thus they emphasize an elitist element that is alien to our social temper. The deeper elitism of all intellectual activity is, perhaps fortunately, less open to the public view; were it, the values of the scientific community might be even harder for them to understand.

Of the cultural arguments for the support of science, only the appeal to international competition, and the national prestige involved in scoring high, seems to have enough potential appeal to serve as at least one element of a basis for support. Since we are already supporting our entries in this Olympiad from the public purse, appeals to national prestige may help keep the process going; even if, alone, they would be hardly sufficient to initiate it.

The pyramid-building arguments for Federal support of science and learning contain an important germ of potential truth. They rest on what economists would call stagnationist views about the underlying forces of growth in our economy. Essentially, these reflect an estimate that, in the absence of special stimuli—a war, a postwar re-equipment boom, a baby boom and its consequent school and housing construction boom—the forces of growth in our economy are too weak to keep the system at or near its full-employment potential, and therefore some special effort of government policy is required in this direction. The validity of this position is an important open question, on which professional views are divided. So far, so good for scientific pyramidology. The rub, however, is in assuming that there is something unique that science and learning provide in the way of pyramid-building that cannot otherwise be provided. And here again, we come, inevitably, to the value question: Is science a better form of pyramid-building? In whose eyes? If indeed the need to build some kind of pyramid exists, there will be a surplus and not a shortage of candidates, and the choice will be determined by the values of the community as they are registered in the political process. In this process supersonic transports have already shown themselves stronger candidates than accelerators, and it appears unlikely that the values of science and learning will come out on top.

To sum up, then, I have asserted that none of the three rationales that have been offered for continued public support of science and learning on a large and growing scale combines the virtues of intellectual validity and political appeal. The lack of political appeal of some of these rationales is, I think, reasonably clear, and if so, its consequences need hardly be argued. However, the lack of intellectual validity in the arguments used to support a public program does not obviously lead directly to its elimination. If it did, the Federal budget would already be a good deal smaller. But the continuance of programs with obviously weak rationales rests on the political power of interest groups which they benefit. The fact that the national defense rationale for the maritime subsidy program is disowned by the Department of Defense does not diminish the political power of the U.S. flag ship operators, the ship builders and the maritime unions, so the program continues. For good or ill, the community of academic scientists and scholars does not have those characteristics that give it the potential for an effective lobby. It is too small in numbers, too scattered geographically, least conspicuous in just those states and Congressional districts which produce most of the men of high seniority who hold senior posts in committees and subcommittees of Congress, typically either indifferent to politics or episodically moved by waves of passion focused on issues. Such is not the stuff of which influence on the Congress is made.

However, the political picture must not be painted entirely in dark tones. Natural science, at least, has achieved a considerable institutionalized position within the Executive Branch, both in terms of full-time officials and the structure of part-time advisory positions. The most important elements in this structure are familiar: the position of Science Advisor to the President, which carries with it the chairmanship of both the President's Science Advisory Committee of part-time advisors and that of the Federal Council of Science and Technology of full-time government officials; at least two of the five Commissionerships of the Atomic Energy Commission; the whole top hierarchy of the National Science Foundation; the Directorship of Defense Research and Engineering, which is the third ranking position in that enormous and powerful department; Assistant Secretaries or special assistants to the Secretary for science, research, and technology in several of the other Cabinet Departments; all posts which for the last decade or more have been filled by scientists or ex-scientists, many of whom have had strong academic affiliations.

Every Federal bureaucracy becomes to a greater

or lesser extent a lobby for its own programs, and it is, of course, a strategically placed lobby with special resources of knowledge and access to Congress that give it considerable power.

Thus, despite its limitations as a public pressure group, the natural scientific community has achieved through its position in the Executive some political leverage. The permanence of this power is difficult to judge. Executive agencies with organized clienteles outside the government have great resources of endurance in the processes of bureaucratic competition for funds and organizational status. The Veterans Administration does not become the subordinate branch of the Social Security Administration that a logical view of its functions would make it. The Departments of Commerce and Labor are not merged, no matter how much overlap in their activities is visible to the eye of the budget examiner. But, though the life of government organizations without ties to substantial extra-governmental groups is more chancy, it seems reasonable to venture the speculation that the place of science in the Executive Branch of Government is secure enough to offset in part its weakness as a public pressure group. This in turn supports the conjecture that arguments and political pressures not strong enough to achieve continued growth in Federal programs of support

may still exert enough force to keep these programs going at something like their recent scale,
with perhaps a factor of growth more similar to
that of other "old" programs than the striking
increases of the past.

If the prospects for increasing Federal support
of academic research in the natural sciences on a
lavish scale are poor, those for the social sciences
and humanities are correspondingly less bright.
While some growth in both from their present low
levels is reasonably to be expected, it does not appear to me that they can ever generate the kind
of support, even in relation to their much smaller
costs, than the natural sciences have already
achieved.

The difficulty of the natural sciences is that they
are growing too expensive. The social sciences labor
under the worse handicap of always verging on the
subversive, and especially so when they deal
with acute and difficult current problems. In the
humanities, the gap between academic and popular standards is at least as large as the gap between the scientists and the public understanding
of science, and the supposed fruits in technology
are not available to help conceal it.

If the prospects for maintaining the pace of
growing public support for science and learning
are as poor as I have pictured them, what about

the support for other functions of higher education, and especially the university. By contrast, these appear to me to be much brighter.

In particular, the demand for more and more widely available higher education as the ever-wider door to individual opportunity accords squarely with the strongest, most widely-held, and most persistent sentiments of the mass of the American public. It appeals to the whole of the actual and potential middle class, which means almost the whole of the politically effective community of the United States.

The strength of this appeal and the political power of those to whom it is addressed are seen in the remarkable and steady growth of publicly-financed systems of higher education. Three quarters of the threefold growth in total enrollments since the Second World War has been in public institutions. At the beginning of the period public and private institutions were about equal in total enrollments; today, the former are twice as big as the latter. This growth has been financed in great part by a system of taxation—in the states—which by and large bears more heavily on the lower income groups whose children do not go to college in large numbers, than on the middle and upper income groups whose children do. In a democratic society with a strong ideological commitment to egalitarian values, this is a striking piece of history.

The financial capacity of the states has increasingly been strained by still rising enrollments and unit costs, and that of the private institutions even more so. Pressures for more Federal support accordingly have grown. The support which is responsive to these pressures has been measured in terms either of enrollment or potential increase in enrollment, which correspond to the training and socialization functions most broadly defined. In the last several fiscal years, support of this kind has grown sharply, at the same time that the pace of increase in the support of science has slowed down. Programs to support new construction of academic facilities and to provide scholarships and student loans, which constituted a little more than five per cent of the total Federal support of universities and colleges in 1963 and 1964, had grown to over twenty per cent by 1965, and just short of thirty per cent by 1966, the last year for which complete figures are available. The current budget proposals, reflecting the pressures of the war, provide for no great increase in last year's figures. But the political potential for future growth in these programs appears very high indeed, and some form of regular Federal grant to every recognized institution of higher education, the magnitude of which is based on a combination of enrollments and their growth, appears to be a likely form for this program to take.

The other sphere of academic activity which appears to have a high potential for further public support is the combination of training experts and participating in the application of academic knowledge and expertise to the solution of practical problems in the larger society. These are more the sphere of the university than of the whole system of higher education. Both exhibit a direct practical utility that escapes the necessity of explanation in terms of conversion to more useful ends more readily seen. The utility of the expert need be judged by no more subtle criterion than his ability to command a job. The value of specialized higher training is clearly being endorsed by the market, and many occupations which were once thought to be well-filled by those with some general education, who would then learn by doing on the job, increasingly seek the applicants whose fitness is attested by a diploma or certificate. Even schools of public administration and government have no difficulty in filling their classrooms and finding employment for their graduates. Similarly, the business of university involvement in practical problem-solving meets something like a crude market test, since it is financed in substantial part on a contract basis. Its buyers are mainly instrumentalities of government, who are paying for expert help out of their program budgets, rather than out of funds marked for the support of science and learning.

To point out that these activities meet a market test in a direct way that the cultivation of science and learning does not, is not to say that their claims to superior utility need be taken at face value. Rather it is simply to observe that the question of what justifies the continuance of these activities is in the one case answered *ipso facto* in terms of a criterion which our society accepts, whereas on the other, that answer must be generated *ad hoc*.

How a growth of advanced training in various professional and technical subjects will be supported financially remains a problem. Some of it will be covered by the kind of formulae based on enrollments and growth that I have suggested above as the likely forms of general support. To the extent that particular kinds of advanced training are greatly more expensive than other kinds of education, because they require expensive facilities, or large amounts of the time of highly paid instructors per student, or both, as in the case for example in medicine, special support programs are likely.

Traditionally, graduate programs in professional disciplines have not offered much in the way of scholarship aid for students; and law and medical degrees were available chiefly to those who could afford to forego income over a long period as well as pay tuitions and living costs. Heavy federal support for graduate training in the natural sciences and engineering has undermined this tradition somewhat. A likely form of future support for graduate training is some kind of loan program, probably incorporating a subsidy element for at least some of its users. But in any event, the presence, in no matter how imperfect a form, of some kind of market test of the usefulness of the results is what makes the prospects of rising public support in these areas of application brighter than it is for science and learning itself.

The near-term future I have pictured for the American universities, in sum, shows the following shifts in emphasis. There will be increasing public and especially federal support for higher education in general, probably based on some kind of formulae emphasizing numbers and growth. There will also be increasing growth in public support for advanced professional and technical training. This will be combined with a continued or even increased growth in the practical involve-

67

ments of the universities in applying expert knowledge to practical problems.

On the other hand, there will be a substantial slowing of the growth in direct public support of academic science and learning. Within this total, it is likely that the now small share going to the social sciences will increase somewhat, and the minuscule public support for the humanities will also grow more. Concretely, this will mean less money given directly to professors for assistants, time-off from teaching to do research, travel and the like. Large expensive items of research equipment will be harder to come by. The most spectacular and expensive items, such as new accelerators and telescopes, will probably be built at a slower pace than they have been over the past two decades.

How the universities in general, and the community of scientists and scholars in particular will respond to these changes is a matter for speculation, and a wide range of answers is possible.

One general adaptation may be some rediscovery of virtue in the earlier position of the higher learning in the university, where its role was more auxiliary to the central functions of teaching and training. A shift in that direction from the present position may further result in some diminution in the present emphasis by the academic community on the training of scientists and scholars, and a willingness to accord higher value to the training of applied scientists and experts of all sorts. Not every professor of physics will feel that the measure of his success is how many Ph.D.'s in high energy particle physics he has turned out who have, themselves, become professors of physics who . . . , and so on ad infinitum.

The shift from project grants and fellowships to general support for institutions and students will do something to increase the powers of university administrators relative to those of academic departments and individual professors, again reversing the process of the post-war period. But the reversal will be very far from complete and the position of the professional guild and its individual members will remain strong. Their central position as the judges of professional competence and the certifiers of advanced training, in a situation of growing demands for higher degrees and advanced training will ensure that strength.

To the extent that new forms of Federal support will go more to the institution and less to the individual professors, the processes of competition for funds will move inside the institutions themselves, from its present locus in the executive agencies and the Congress. Here the arguments which have little appeal in the public forum may

69

be more powerful, and the lobbying strength that academicians lack in the governmental area is theirs in plenitude when it is against trustees, presidents, directors, and deans that they must lobby.

Put differently, the demand for the services of the academic guild as a whole will remain strong even though it is expressed in different terms than it has been recently. How the rewards for meeting that demand are divided up among its members will depend more on the balance of bargaining forces within the academy, rather than in the larger society.

Yet, whatever the outcome, the volume of resources directly available for the support of scientific and scholarly activity will probably grow more slowly.

Inevitably, there will be slower growth in the level of scientific and scholarly activity. How much this will slow down the growth of knowledge itself is a harder question, that I will not attempt to anwer. Those who point, correctly, to the very high proportion of good work in every field produced by a relatively small fraction of those at work in it, sometimes deduce, incorrectly, I think, that the diminution of support will not affect the results at all. This argument overlooks the effect of the wider spread of activity in recruiting men into the field; more thousands of graduate students does increase somewhat the chances of finding the few in a thousand who will do something significant.

How much this slowdown in direct support does affect the degree to which able men are recruited, encouraged, and permitted to work within the academy does depend very much on the way the academic community responds to the shifting nature of its public support, how broadly the possible responses are defined, who chooses among them, and under what stimuli and pressures. But in these matters, the academic community cannot merely await events, they must seize them.

3

AN AFTERWORD

A T THIS WRITING, nine months after the two lectures which constitute the first two chapters of this book were given, developments in the growth and finance of higher education underline the arguments they presented. Student enrollments are already growing at a faster pace than the Office of Education's projections made less than two years ago indicated. Cuts in total Federal expenditures on civilian programs that the Congress has required as the price of a temporary tax increase have substantially halted the growth of Federal expenditures in support of academic science. Yet, by contrast, some other kinds of support for higher education, especially programs of student aid, have been exempted from limitations on expenditures from funds already appropriated, underlining the differential political appeal of these two aspects of the universities' activities. The sense of financial crisis in higher education has become more widespread; this is

75

especially the case with respect to the private universities. Academic administrators and their organizations have correspondingly increased their calls for Federal aid. At this moment, with a new administration taking office between the time these words are written and they appear, it would be extraordinarily rash to predict the specific response of the Federal Government to such requests. Yet it does appear safe to say that expanded programs of Federal aid will not come without lively examination of both old programs and new proposals, and that, accordingly, the scrutiny of the present mode and rationale of government support for science which was anticipated in the lectures will come sooner rather than later.

However, this afterword has not been written simply to reaffirm the arguments and convictions already sufficiently displayed and defended above. Rather it is to offer a few lines to point out one possible path of change which would enable American higher education and especially its central institutions—the universities—to reconcile the basis on which the public, through the Federal treasury, is willing to furnish support with their own purposes in cultivating science and learning.

The growth in college enrollments, both in absolute numbers and in proportion of each age cohort entering, reflects a number of different social demands. The most important is the increasingly widespread belief in education as an avenue of social mobility, in a society in which occupational and locational change are all-pervasive, and social mobility is accordingly a fact of life for the vast majority of families. Almost as important is the increasing reliance on certification through formal education of some "higher" kind as the primary channel into many of the wide spectrum of occupational activities above the blue collar level that include a growing proportion of the labor force. This in turn partly results from the increase in the complexity and variety of ideas, information, and techniques that must be mastered for these jobs, making extended formal training the appropriate means of preparation. Partly, however, it reflects a broader tendency to substitute formal education for informal on-the-job training, and to professionalize many activities and occupations without close regard for either the necessity or the appropriateness of the education offered as training for them.

To perform these functions of socialization and certification in what we have defined above as a true university—one in which the central concern of the faculty is with science and learning and the training of scholars and scientists—is becoming increasingly difficult and expensive. Students' stri-

dent demands for more "relevance" in the curricu-
lum is a characteristic symptom of the difficulty.
Its source lies in the divergence of purpose between the faculty whose interests are in advancing
the frontiers of their specialties and the students
who at most want the training and more typically
the certification that college education provides.
The expense reflects the rapid growth of new
specializations in many disciplines, and the corresponding increase in numbers required for a faculty that "covers" adequately the fields of knowledge, the increasing needs for elaborate equipment
in the sciences, and the rise in faculty salaries oc-
casioned by the rapid growth in their number in
the whole of higher education, in the face of a
more slowly growing supply of qualified people.

The college, not the university, is the appropriate institution for performing the functions of
socialization and certification for the representative
student. If colleges are organized and staffed for
their teaching functions, their costs can be much
lower than those of universities whose main tasks
lie elsewhere. This is already what is happening to
some extent. The demand for student places has
outstripped the capacity of the old universities to
offer them in the old way; so that either newly expanded institutions, such as the state colleges or
newly organized or expanded branches of state uni-

78

versities at new locations fill the need. These are not universities in the proper sense, but the problem for the future is that many of them will strive to become such, in response to pressures from their faculties and administrations, who in turn will seek to copy the models that dominate the graduate schools in which they were trained. It is only by denying these impulses that costs of the new scale of college training can be kept within bounds. But more than this needs to be done. The present universities should, to the greatest possible extent, abandon the function of undergraduate socialization and certification to institutions primarily engaged in them, and reserve their own efforts for higher levels of training, the tasks of adapting scientific and technical knowledge to the solution of difficult social problems, and those of the creation of new knowledge and incorporation of it into the existing body of learning. Their efforts should be aimed at the million graduate and professional students expected a decade hence, rather than the eight or nine times as numerous candidates for first degrees; and at the kind of research at both the more abstract and the more applied ends of the spectrum that can appropriately be related to their education. Even here, the aim of the universities should be to resist rather than broaden demands for increasing certification and for the conversion of every occupation whose practice involves any significant intellectual content into a specialized profession requiring an appropriately specialized course of graduate study. The opposite course would work against the possibility of maintaining the central position of the intellectual concerns of the faculty in shaping the work of the university, and increase its dependence on professional associations whose impulses and aims were heavily trade union in character. Indeed, freed of their direct connection with the task of dealing with undergraduates, the universities may be able to make a searching examination of the relation between the whole structure of post-secondary education and the appropriate and necessary technical training for occupational roles in our society which has been conspicuously lacking to date.

The experience of the two postwar decades makes it clear that the public will pay for the certification and training of its young, activities which respond to needs felt throughout the major part of society. Indeed, we can hazard the guess that the building and staffing of colleges may well be the Federal highway program of the seventies and, once under way, may be as difficult to stop. Research and scholarship are hardly in a similar position.

The support of research and scholarship can

80

then be justified primarily in terms of their role in advanced training and their indispensability in maintaining the kind of institutions that can both provide advanced and specialized training, and assist society in applying knowledge to social problems. As we have already observed, this rationale is no more capable of justifying a particular level or rate of growth of support for scholarship and science than the rationale of direct benefit through technology. However, it associates the support of science and learning with the support of activities performed by the same institutions and to a substantial degree the same people as are engaged in other and more comprehensible purposes. The appropriate mix of the several elements within the institution then becomes the kind of question that can best be left to the experts, e.g. to the academic institutions themselves. The situation would be parallel with respect to the technological-benefit rationale for the support of science only if basic work in science was performed and supported within the organizations—industrial and military laboratories and the like—that themselves were responsible for the development and application of new technology. But of course this is not the case, and precisely because it is not, the issue of the proper relation between the magnitudes of the two kinds of activities moves into the political sphere of decision, rather than remaining with the managers of these organizations and their technical advisors.

This change in the explicit rationale for the support of science would have the further advantage that it would apply more broadly to the higher learning, and cover the social sciences and the humanities more readily than the direct benefit arguments now widely used. To be sure, with more popular and, in aggregate, much more expensive forms of support for higher education at all levels, the claims of academic science and learning will sound less clearly than they have in the recent past. Further, the necessity of justifying the scale of effort by relating it to the magnitude of the universities' responsibilities to the wider society for training and for direct applications of knowledge to society's problems will itself place a limit on these claims. Not all will be loss, however, for in exchange science and learning may be allowed to resume a more protected role, in which they do not seek and are not asked to provide a direct social utility which can be measured in the scales of cost-effectiveness by the executive branch and the legislators to whom it must respond.

A NOTE ON SOURCES

THE LITERATURE on science and public policy is already vast, and the works listed below are meant to do no more than introduce the problems of the field.

The statistical materials on education and Federal support of science are drawn from the publications of the Office of Education and the National Science Foundation. In particular, the *Digest of Educational Statistics for 1966*, and *Projections of Educational Statistics for 1975-76*, also issued in 1966, were the sources on figures for education, and the projections of enrollment. The annual volumes of the N.S.F. publication Federal Funds for Research, Development, and Other Scientific Activities were the chief source for figures on Federal support of science. Also useful were two special NSF publications: *Federal Support to Universities and Colleges, Fiscal Years 1963-66*, (1967) and *National Patterns of R. & D. Resources, 1953-68* (1967).

On the general character of recent relations between science and government in the United States two essays by Don K. Price are particularly helpful: *Government and Science* (New York University Press, 1954), and *The Scientific Estate* (Harvard University Press, 1965).

A sample of the discussion on the justification for Federal support of pure science is provided by the volume entitled *Basic Research and National Goals*, a report to the Committee on Science and Astronautics of the U.S. House of Representatives by the National Academy of Sciences (1965). A parallel document entitled *Applied Science and Technological Progress* was produced in a similar way in 1967. The best general introductions to the rapidly growing economic literature are *Technology, Economic Growth and Public Policy*, R. R. Nelson, M. J. Peck, and E. R. Kalacheck (Brookings, 1967) and *The Economics of Technical Change*, E. Mansfield (W. W. Norton, 1968).

An excellent survey article on university organization in different countries with useful bibliographical footnotes is "Universities and Academic Systems in Modern Societies" by J. Ben-David and A. Zloczower in *Archiv. europ. Sozial. 1962*, pp. 45-84. Its conclusions with respect to the effectiveness of the modes of support for science and learning in the U.S. are somewhat at variance with my own.

The letter, editorial, and news columns of *Science* are prime sources for the attitudes and arguments of the American scientific community in immediate response to current changes in government policy. Examples of somewhat more formal exposition of such views are provided by G. Pake, "Basic Research and the Financial Crisis of the Universities," *Science*, 4 August 1967; P. Handler, "Academic Science and the Federal Government," *ibid.*, 8 September 1967; and L. A. DuBridge, "University Basic Research," *ibid.*, 11 August 1967.

Since these lectures were delivered, a penetrating discussion of the American academic scene by Christopher Jencks and David Riesman, *The Academic Revolution* (Doubleday and Co., 1968) has appeared, which views that scene from a perspective quite similar to my own.